Awaken the Christ Consciousness within You

by Barbara Wilson

edited by Robert Evans Wilson, Jr.

cover art by Kevin Tester

ISBN-10: 0615748740

ISBN-13: 978-0615748740

DEDICATION

To my husband, Bob, for his constant and unfailing encouragement as I endeavored to put into words the very personal experiences of my quest.

Barbara Wilson

ACKNOWLEDGMENTS

This book was originally titled *The Warranty to Live*. The author got the idea for that title from her daughter, Cynthia Wilson.

CONTENTS

Preface   vii

Foreword   ix

1   Introduction   11

2   A New Understanding   16

3   Effective Prayer   22

4   Be Still and Know   36

5   The Still Small Voice   51

6   The Gift of Healing   63

7   Epilogue   76

8   Suggested Reading   86

Barbara Wilson

EDITOR'S PREFACE

by Robert Evans Wilson, Jr.

This book, which was written by my mother in 1974, was lost and forgotten for 38 years. Since it had not been published, I assumed it was never completed. Then I found it a few months ago. It was complete; there was also a foreword written by a prominent proponent of the power of prayer; plus she had a letter of introduction to an editor with a book publishing company. After reading this book, I was moved to publish it. First to honor my mother, who passed away in 1991, and second to share the wisdom she discovered on her spiritual journey.

Although, she never uses the term, this is a book about the Law of Attraction written from a Christian perspective. This story is a chronicle of my mother's spiritual journey, and how that journey took her from a life of fear and sadness to a life of peace and joy. This is the story of how she acquired an understanding of God's gifts to man, and how to use them. She wrote this book in order to share those gifts with you.

In the years leading up to her writing this book, she was a frequent guest on several radio shows and a keynote speaker to many conferences around the United States. To those audiences, she shared the information in this book.

I have inserted some "Editor's Notes" here and there throughout the book to expand the background information which I believe enriches her story, and demonstrates more fully the profound miracles she experienced as a result of prayer.

Barbara Wilson

FOREWORD

by William R. Parker

As one reads these chapters of Barbara Wilson's first book, you are immediately struck with the simplicity, clarity, and forthrightness of her approach. In a day of false sophistication, this is refreshing to have something presented to us that we can immediately grasp, and has meaning for us.

In a day where despair is so widespread, she shares with us her pilgrimage, her own despair and how she moved out of it into trust and faith. She holds out the hope for others, if they will but begin the search.

She moves logically into healing, which in my opinion, is the wave of the future. Barbara is on solid ground here, and calls us all to explore, and get in touch with the Divinity within, and to release it within our lives so we can be healed and made whole.

Further, she calls upon us to personalize God by looking at Jesus the Christ. Jesus helps us to personalize God. This is how Jesus approached people: "He healed all who came." "Love one another as I have loved you." "I have come that you might have life and have it more abundantly." "My peace I give unto you."

So there is a New Life for all of us if we begin the search. If we would go into the closet (our own mind) and close the door, and pray and meditate, we could be renewed, revitalized and healed, and made whole.

I recommend this book to all who are seekers. It is an honest book. It challenges us anew, and we begin the journey to find the way, the truth, and the light for ourselves.

William R. "Cherry" Parker, 1914-1993, was a psychologist, minister, and the founder of Community Church by the Bay in Newport Beach, California. He was best known for melding psychological testing, group counseling and prayer therapy. He was co-author of the best-selling books *Prayer Can Change Your Life* and *Man's Greatest Single Problem*. He also wrote *Pathology of Speech*.

1 INTRODUCTION

If it can happen to me, it can happen to you. As I look back on the panorama of my life, I can hardly believe it. It is an absolute miracle. If anyone had told me that life could be this way, I would have quickly said, "No way, it is just not possible."

A series of rather tragic events actually began my seeking after a meaning and a purpose for life, although I was completely unaware of it at the time. This desire has led me toward finding both a new Barbara and a marvelous life along a spiritual path.

The following events, if taken singly, may not be regarded by some as tragic, but in the collective manner in which they occurred, they brought an absolutely traumatic state of mind to me.

My husband, Bob, and I had just returned from college and had set up housekeeping in our first real home. He had graduated from Emory University and I had completed my studies of radiological technology and was now a full-fledged X-ray technician. Life was really beginning, I thought, and I was quite excited over the prospects of finding happiness at last! We were back in the city where we both grew up, Savannah, Georgia. My husband had his first job, and I had mine as an X-ray technician at nearby Camp Stewart. How many lives have started out just this way?

Ours was certainly not to progress as we had dreamed and planned.

All afternoon of the first Christmas Eve back home, I felt uneasy and did not know why. As I made last minute preparations I was far less than excited. I called my parents and everything seemed alright even though my alcoholic father had taken to the bed with his bottle. This was not unusual but I remained deeply concerned about him.

Bob and I had gone out for a special Christmas Eve dinner together, but I was unable to enjoy the evening. A sense of impending doom possessed me, and I seemed to be waiting for something to happen. Throughout my childhood, I had occasions when I would have a feeling of what was to come. This intuition or inner knowing is actually the voice of God and of truth. The foreboding I now experienced was new to me; I was sure it involved my parents and was equally as sure that it would be something tragic.

At three a.m. the next morning a neighbor of my parents came to our home to inform me of my mother's death. She had died in her sleep of a heart attack at age forty-seven; there was no history of heart condition.

At this point in my young life, I was fraught with fear. Fear literally stalked my path. Certainly fear is a common emotion in young people as the complexities of life are experienced for the first time. My fear, however, was as much a part of me as breathing. Fear seemed to center around security, but I actually feared life itself.

There seemed to be no rhyme or reason to life. Why was there so much unhappiness and suffering? This was all that I had ever known, and I could not understand what life was all about. Nevertheless, life continued on in the same negative pattern in spite of me. This was the beginning of the many crises that I now refer to as rocks and boulders that were placed in my path for my emotional and spiritual growth; they have helped me to become more and more the person I believe God intended me to be.

First, I had an early miscarriage; the result, I believe, of all the negative emotions that I had experienced since my mother's untimely death; next I had to commit my father to the psychiatric ward of Candler Hospital after he, in a drunken stupor, had set the house on fire; and then Bob was admitted to the VA hospital in Augusta, Georgia with moderately advanced tuberculosis.

Here I was at the age of twenty, being forced by circumstances to come to grips with life.

I was extremely resentful that we were suffering all these misfortunes while our friends were buying homes and having babies. All the normal things that young married couples experience were being denied us, and I hated it. I handled none of these crises adequately. My emotions daily ran the gauntlet of negativity. The only joy and happiness that I experienced during those years of crises was the birth of our children, which was six years after the problems began. It was five months after the birth of our daughter that the last crisis came: my husband was dying of glomerular nephritis, a fatal kidney disease.

With this, my world fell down around me. I finally faced the fact that something had to give. Either there was a better way, or I could not continue the battle of life. I was ready to throw in the towel.

It has been said that those who really seek the truth are those who have their backs to the wall, who find themselves at the end of their rope. I had been a Christian all of my life; I had attended Sunday School and church regularly. Where was the faith I was taught to rely on? Without a religious faith to strengthen me, what in the world would I do? God obviously did not love me and had absolutely no concern for my welfare as I had been taught that He did. With this rude awakening, I felt utterly lost and alone, a victim of cruel fate.

Through a great miracle, a spiritual happening that I describe later, in Chapter Four: The Still, Small Voice, a door was opened onto a whole new world that I had never dreamed existed.

It is my belief that since all of us are a part of God and His universe, anything that I experience emotionally, others also experience. Therefore, we all can glean from one another as we travel through this earth life. I am writing of my experiences with the hope that they will benefit others in a spiritual way... that you also will find purpose, joy, and peace. The popular song, People, where Barbra Streisand sings, "People who need people are the luckiest people in the world," is aptly put for we surely do need each other. As we learn to relate to people, we are actually learning to relate to God - - even when we are not conscious of this experience.

Editor's Note: *Mother writes that she was filled with fear, and that fear ruled her life. I would like to share with you an extreme* example of how fearful she was. When she was in her early twenties, my father was hospitalized with tuberculosis for a year. During that time, Mother, who was medically trained as an x-ray technician, could not understand why she had not contracted his disease. Her fear of catching it was so great, that she worried about it constantly. Within a few months, it seemed that she had indeed attracted the illness for she began to show TB symptoms. However, when given the test for TB, it came back negative. Despite the negative test result, her symptoms were so profound that her doctor admitted her to a TB sanatorium. While there, she continued to test negative. Nevertheless, her fear continued to mount until one morning she woke up blind. There was no medical reason for her to be blind, but for several days she had no vision. Eventually it came back. The doctors diagnosed it as hysterical blindness. I share this story to show you how far she traveled in her spiritual journey.

2 A NEW UNDERSTANDING

"For if a man is in Christ he becomes a new person altogether the past is finished and gone, everything has become fresh and new" II Cor. 5l7 Phillips

Life is difficult but it is supposed to be, for there are lessons to be learned that will help us grow and mature. The very nature of the earth planet is such that we expect to be met with problems and adversity. However, it is through just such circumstances that the opportunity for growth on all levels is given.

In reality, problems are blessings when they are a challenge and a motivation to rise above the problems and forge ahead with faith and hope. Life is like a school, and in every situation we are given the opportunity to pass or to fail. Shakespeare said in "As You Like It", "All the world's a stage and all the men and women merely players." If our proper role is found, i.e., the purpose for our lives, then life will become exciting and every day an adventure. Too few people ever realize that there is a purpose for their lives, so they stumble and fall throughout life wondering what it is all about. They are ridden with fear, anxiety, hate, hostility, and negative attitudes that precipitate more of the same. These people never seem to realize that it does not have to be that way.

There was a time, in fact, a better part of my life, when I lived right there not knowing there was a purpose for the circumstances in my life. Fear was my constant companion, and the day I was able to cast out fear was the day I knew freedom for the very first time and this was only a small degree of what was yet to be experienced.

Far more than is realized now, even with all the books written on the power of positive thinking, wholeness and health are primarily dependent on our state of mind. What an incentive for a healthy body to pursue freedom of mind. For when there is mental and emotional health the result is physical health. This is found through looking within, getting to know self, recognizing the negatives and casting them out. It is never easy but there is nothing in the world that is more important. Here God's Kingdom within is discovered and lives change. We do become as Paul said, "...a new person altogether - - the past is finished and gone, everything has become fresh and new" (II Cor. 5:17 Phillips). These are not mere words, this is a truth that can be anyone's just for the asking and searching.

We are not alone in our journey through life or in those moments of desperation that all experience at one time or another when there is confusion, and loneliness, and a wondering why we are beset with so many problems. God is ever seeking to gain our attention, but we are so absorbed in our own little world that we are not aware of the subtle prompts of our Creator. If we hear at all, we call it a hunch or a coincidence and never realize that it is God ever trying to pervade our consciousness. Like a radio that is plugged into the electrical outlet but not tuned to the station, the message is garbled and makes no sense. This is the way it is when we are not tuned into the Source of our being.

How is God heard in this busy work-a-day world, through our frustrations and never ending problems? Meditation is the key to God, to the real self, and to finding the Kingdom within as Jesus Christ promised. There is nothing more rewarding than daily meditation; it frees the soul and brings a balance to the mental, physical, and spiritual life. Then God's promises are experienced - - the joy and peace that passes all understanding.

Prayer is talking to God; meditation is listening to God. Divine guidance is there for the taking. It is ever present, but it is necessary to stop and listen for that still, small voice, This is the only real protection to be found in an uncertain world. The feeling of peace within is one very real assurance that He is with us, omnipresence becomes a reality.

"Be still and know that I am God" (Psalms 46:10 KJV).

This is the way. It will change lives. We will become the person we have always wanted to be deep within. The real self, the Spiritual self - - that spark of God that is the very essence of the soul - - will be Awakened. Paul said, "...it is sown a natural body; it is raised a spiritual body - - as there is a natural body so will there be a spiritual body" (I Cor. I5:44 Phillips). It is necessary to develop our spiritual selves if we are really ever to know God and to have a whole and balanced life. This occurs when inner peace is experienced, even to a small degree. Christ assured us that "I am with you always even to the end of the world" Matthew 28:20 Phillips).

So much time is spent nourishing the physical body, adorning it with beautiful clothes and fussing over diets and exercises. All of this is very important as the physical body is the vehicle in this physical world and the temple of the living God, but what is done for the spiritual body? I would chance to say that many are unaware that there is a spiritual body to consider.

We would never plan a trip without making some form of itinerary or schedule. But what preparation has been made for the trip back home when there is a physical death and a passing into the next dimension; the world of spirit that is called heaven? Going to church once a week is important to the total well being, but it is not enough preparation. In the worship service there is praise and glory and thanksgiving to God for all the many blessings, but it is only in individual seeking and studying that spiritual growth is experienced. We do not suddenly become saints when we pass over; growth is continued and built upon what has been started here. How much easier and more glorious it will be later when spiritual growth is started here and now.

It is not necessary to understand the science of the unknown world, but it is necessary to be aware that there are spiritual laws that govern life. The unseen, the Infinite Invisible, is all around. It is the only real reality. What appears to be reality in human eyes is not always what it appears to be. It is only necessary to understand ourselves, our ultimate destiny and the purpose for this earth life. When spiritual development is accomplished, preparation has been made for the heavenly life, and a little bit of heaven is established right here on Earth.

This is why Christ Jesus came to show the Way. For the Christian world, Jesus of Nazareth is the Master and Savior, and it is through the application of His teachings that the way, truth and life are found. He promised the abundant life when we seek God first; this is an absolute truth that I have found on the spiritual path.

God knew how difficult it would be without the light of His love to direct our lives. How foolish not to grasp this truth and thus receive the gift of inner harmony and peace. Our environment then becomes harmonious and peaceful, to that degree which we allow it through inner illumination. The choice is ours, to find God within through meditation, and to experience the excitement of life; or go through this earth phase of existence filled with fear, doubt, and frustration.

When we live anxious, up-tight lives, maximum potential is never realized. Our life should be like an organ when all the stops are pulled out; what a glorious sound! The organ is giving all that it has. The same is true with our lives; when we learn to pull out all the stops there is no limit to what can be accomplished, potential has no bounds. God is literally "let loose." Life has no limitations.

To put faith in the material things of this world, whether it be in possessions, jobs, or people, is to build for ourselves a state of insecurity. The things of this material world come and go; they are constantly changing. It is only the spiritual world that is constant and unchanging. Within all of us is a deep yearning and a loneliness that we try to quiet and satisfy with things: superficial excitement, trips, cars, houses, mink coats, boats, and so on. Our closets are literally filled with things, and it is wondered at times when we rediscover them, 'Why did I buy that?" Fibber McGee's closet is symbolic of this. Remember that every time he opened the door there was an avalanche of "things?" When the Divine nature is unknown, things tend to overcome us. We tend to cling to the material world seeking to find that which can only be found through Christ. The world of materialism has never brought peace within or without, and it never will.

There is a song that says, "When the party's over, then come the tears." When the excitement dies down, when the party is over, the yearning is still there. Why? Because through it all God has tried to get our attention and we have not responded. Our souls are crying out for God, the very essence of our being. This is because we are spiritual beings living only a physical life. The physical body is simply a housing on this planet which enables us to benefit from the experiences that only life on earth can offer. Just as the astronauts need special equipment to walk on the moon, so the soul needs a physical body to live on the planet earth. But to live on this planet without the experience of God is absolutely devastating. Experiencing God is not difficult; it only takes a deep desire and a commitment which allows the opportunity for a personal encounter with God. The first spiritual experience of my quest really made the difference in my seeking more deeply for a new life and so it is with everyone. With the very first spiritual or mystical experience, the veil drops, the eyes open, and it truly is the beginning of a whole new, exciting experience.

3 EFFECTIVE PRAYER

"Whatever you pray about and ask for, believe that you have received it, and it will be yours"

Mark 11:24 Phillips

Editor's Note: *I would like to elaborate on the story of the miracle of my father's kidney transplant. It was a genuine answer to my mother's prayers, and an event that began her spiritual journey.*

My recollection of those days is sparse. I was three years old. What I do recall is that my strong Daddy was no longer able to pick me up and hold me. He spent many days home from work; never getting out of bed. My mother took over all the driving, and I recall her having to stop on occasion for my father to vomit on the side of the road.

When Dad was diagnosed with kidney failure, Mother prayed for his healing. Against all the medical opinions that there was no way that he would live, she prayed for a miracle. In the meantime, on their doctor's advice, who had said my father had less than a year to live, my parents began planning for his death.

They sold the house they owned and used the proceeds to build a three-unit apartment house with the plan that my mother, my sister and I would live in one unit, and live on the income from the other two units. They knew that would not be enough, so my mother, having been a housewife and stay-home Mom, returned to her work as an x-ray technician. Initially, because my father needed her care, she took only temporary positions. Those temporary jobs were to bring in needed income, to help update her skills, and to develop a network from which she could later find permanent employment. The plan was, that once the inevitable day came and my father passed away, she would work part time until my sister and I were old enough to go school. Then she would go to work full time. All during this time, she continued to pray regularly for my father's healing.

One of the amazing (to me) choices my parents made during this time of extreme stress, was to have another child. At the time of my father's diagnosis, I was an only child. They did not want me to grow up alone, so knowing that my father was living under a death sentence, they decided to get pregnant with my sister. As I look back on this decision it seems incredibly unselfish to me that my mother would take on the tremendous burden of a second child knowing that she was to become a single mother. It is a decision, for which I am eternally grateful because my sister has become my closest friend and confidant.

My mother and father's first miracle came while my mother was working at one of those temporary x-ray jobs. There was some down time at the doctor's office where she was working. She went into the waiting room to look for something to read on the magazine rack. She glanced at all the popular magazines of the

day, but passed over them when she saw on the bottom shelf a
several months out of date medical journal. She felt guided to that
publication, so she picked it up and began to read.

Before long, she was reading an article about a physician, Joseph
Edward Murray who was doing some experimental surgery at
Peter Bent Brigham hospital in Boston, Massachusetts. The
surgery he was performing was the world's first organ transplants.
The organ he was transplanting was the kidney. She began to get
excited about what she was reading and plowed deeper into the
article. She read that he was looking for volunteers, but there was
a catch. The volunteer had to have an identical twin. Back in 1960,
there were no anti-rejection drugs, so they had to have a perfect
match. My father happened to have an identical twin. At that
point, my mother had to know if they were still looking for
volunteers. She got on the phone and dialed Boston until she
reached the doctor. He said, "Yes, we are still looking for
volunteers. Please send me your husband and his brother."

That night my mother and father went to visit my Uncle Ralph.
When he heard the news, his reply was immediate, "To save your
life; yes you can have one of my kidneys!"

They made their plans to go to Boston. There would be several
visits before the surgery would be performed. During one of those
first visits, the doctors needed to determine if my father and his
brother were indeed identical. There was no DNA testing back
then, so what they did was a skin graft from my uncle to my
father. When my father's body did not reject the skin graft, they
knew they had a perfect match.

One more crisis arose before the surgery could commence. Uncle
Ralph was recently married, and his wife, Beth, was terrified that

he would die in the surgery. She did not want him to go through with it. Ralph was adamant that he would do it, but eventually she found something that made him hesitate. He was having to take a lot of time off from work, and while it was not costing him any money to be in the hospital with my Dad, there were incidental travel expenses (meals, hotel, airfare) for Beth who went to Boston with him. Plus, with him missing so much work, he was running through his savings and vacation pay. "How are we going to pay the bills each month?" Beth implored. "How are we going to pay all my travel expenses to Boston? We don't know how long we'll be there!"

Uncle Ralph went to my father and asked if he could help with the costs. But, my parents had put all their money into the apartment building. And, with Dad working fewer hours, there was no extra money. It looked like they were going to have to forego the surgery.

Once again, my mother prayed for a miracle. Then one day while she was grocery shopping, there was a display table with a representative from a laundry detergent company asking housewives to enter a contest by writing an advertising jingle for them. Mom dashed one off. As she told me, "I wrote down the first thing that popped into my head." Then she dropped it into the box. Shortly thereafter, she received a letter that she had won the contest. The prize was $1,000.00 which was a small fortune in 1961 (worth around $20,000 in 2012). It was more than enough money to pay Uncle Ralph's bills while he was out of work, and Aunt Beth's travel expenses to Boston. It was another answer to prayer.

The operation was a success, and Dad became the 12th person in the world to have a kidney transplant and live. He went on to live for 18 more years.

These miracles had a profound effect on my mother. Her prayers were answered. Any doubts she may have had about her belief in prayer were gone. Now she became curious why more people didn't know about this. She asked why it worked for her and Dad. She had many more questions and began a spiritual journey to discover the answers. This book is a compilation of what she learned.

There are many, many books written on prayer, but until answered prayer has been in our lives, the full meaning and power of this gift from God cannot be known.

We are here on earth to be met with problems that are designed to strengthen and help us to grow mentally and spiritually, but we are not left alone in this myriad of never ending challenges. The lamp on the table will not function unless it is plugged into the current of electricity. So it is with us. We stymie our true purpose in living if we are not connected with our Creator. The power is there but until it is tapped through effective prayer and meditation, we are not the complete and vital being that God intended.

Most people, I believe, pray in some form or another at some time in their lives. Often in a crisis people finally turn to God when all else has failed. God, who has been there all the time, is usually ignored by His children as they battle their problems in their own consciousness and strength. Perhaps this is because the magnitude of God awes them and they believe that God is "way out yonder somewhere." The childish faith in a God who is taking care of us and who wraps us in His arms has somehow become lost.

Few people truly understand the reality of prayer; that it is a force, a power in the universe to draw upon. A power given to us by a loving God to use as protection, security and comfort. Prayer is not merely a tool to fall back upon only in a crisis, but is to be used daily to aid in successfully meeting the demands of life. I once thought, as I read such words, that it all sounded so beautiful but so totally unrealistic.

It is not necessary to petition God for He already knows our every need. Be assured that He wants more for us then we do for ourselves, His love is unlimited; it knows no bounds, and as we sense the divine Presence, the truth of His all-encompassing love is made clear. As we come into His Presence we experience an "at-one-ment" with God and all His creation.

"I am the vine itself; you are the branches. It is the man who shares my life and whose life I share who proves fruitful. For the plain fact is that apart from me you can do nothing at all" (John 15:5 Phillips). The fifteenth chapter of John has helped me more than any other chapter in the Bible to realize that it is only through the Christ that dwells within me that I am able to find direction and solutions for my problems. The trunk, or vine, of the tree is Christ; we are the branches and thus are one with the trunk. Imagine the branches separated from the trunk; they could not possibly survive. The source of power is invisible within the trunk and the tree draws its nourishment from the earth -- God. All the elements needed for growth are found rooted in the good earth. The vine, branches, and earth are all one. As this parable is applied to our lives, we begin to understand the source of our own life and supply. With this conscious awareness of God, prayers are answered and the abundant life is found.

Jesus said to seek first the Kingdom of God which is within us, then, "all these things shall be added unto you" (Matthew 6:33 KJV). I believe that this means that all things will be added on every level of life. It certainly has been my experience that this is true. Only when the mind that is in Christ Jesus is within us will we be able to rise above everyday problems and experience the healing of our inner conflicts.

We should never attempt to tell God how to rule His world, but more often than not this is exactly the tone of our prayers as we attempt to influence God to do our will. Prayer should be the time that we ask to be shown His will in each situation of life. In the Lord's Prayer, Jesus was showing us how to pray when he said, "Thy will, be done," not our will. When the omniscience, omnipresence, and omnipotence of God is realized, we will cease trying to influence Him. Then prayer life will change. With this new understanding, prayer life will be effective, faith will be strengthened, and the true meaning of living under grace will become a reality.

The question always arises, "Is it proper to pray for material gain, houses, cars, increased income, and so forth?" Our need is God's need from the very moment the need is manifest. I believe that God provides for our every need and it is not necessary to ask; it is only necessary to surrender the problem or situation to Him, and in full faith wait for His answer. Even when the problem appears impossible to our finite eyes, we will see it worked out and in amazement will ask ourselves, "Why did I not think of that?"

I have had people say to me, "Oh, I would never bother God with my everyday problems; He is too busy with more important things." This is the concept that God is way out yonder somewhere. One must understand that He dwells within each of us as a constant source of light, guidance, comfort, and love.

There is nothing more important to God than one of His children. We are a part of God, and being a part of Him, He cares for us just as a parent cares for each of his children. The scripture about the one lost sheep demonstrates this truth, as does the parable of the Prodigal Son.

Luke Chapter 15 (KJV): *1 Then drew near unto him all the publicans and sinners for to hear him. 2 And the Pharisees and scribes murmured, saying, This man receiveth sinners, and eateth with them. 3 And he spake this parable unto them, saying, 4 What man of you, having an hundred sheep, if he lose one of them, doth not leave the ninety and nine in the wilderness, and go after that which is lost, until he find it? 5 And when he hath found it, he layeth it on his shoulders, rejoicing. 6 And when he cometh home, he calleth together his friends and neighbours, saying unto them, Rejoice with me; for I have found my sheep which was lost.*

7 I say unto you, that likewise joy shall be in heaven over one sinner that repenteth, more than over ninety and nine just persons, which need no repentance. 8 Either what woman having ten pieces of silver, if she lose one piece, doth not light a candle, and sweep the house, and seek diligently till she find it? 9 And when she hath found it, she calleth her friends and her neighbours together, saying, Rejoice with me; for I have found the piece which I had lost.

10 Likewise, I say unto you, there is joy in the presence of the angels of God over one sinner that repenteth. 11 And he said, A certain man had two sons: 12 And the younger of them said to his father, Father, give me the portion of goods that falleth to me. And he divided unto them his living. 13 And not many days after the younger son gathered all together, and took his journey into a far country, and there wasted his substance with riotous living. 14 And when he had spent all, there arose a mighty famine in that land; and he began to be in want. 15 And he went and joined himself to a citizen of that country; and he sent him into his fields to feed swine. 16 And he would fain have filled his belly with the husks that the swine did eat: and no man gave unto him. 17 And when he came to himself, he said, How many hired servants of my father's have bread enough and to spare, and I perish with hunger! 18 I will arise and go to my father, and will say unto him, Father, I have sinned against heaven, and before thee, 19 And am no more worthy to be called thy son: make me as one of thy hired servants. 20 And he arose, and came to his father. But when he was yet a great way off, his father saw him, and had compassion, and ran, and fell on his neck, and kissed him. 21 And the son said unto him, Father, I have sinned against heaven, and in thy sight, and am no more worthy to be called thy son. 22 But the father said to his servants, Bring forth the best robe, and put it on him; and put a ring on his hand, and shoes on his feet: 23 And bring hither the fatted calf, and kill it; and let us eat, and be merry: 24 For this my son was dead, and is alive again; he was lost, and is found. And they began to be merry. 25 Now his elder son was in the field: and as he came and drew nigh to the house, he heard music and dancing. 26 And he called one of the servants, and asked what these things meant. 27 And he said unto him, Thy brother is come; and thy father hath killed the fatted calf, because he hath received him safe and sound. 28 And he was angry, and

*would not go in: therefore came his father out, and entreated him.
29 And he answering said to his father, Lo, these many years do I
serve thee, neither transgressed I at any time thy commandment:
and yet thou never gavest me a kid, that I might make merry with
my friends: 30 But as soon as this thy son was come, which hath
devoured thy living with harlots, thou hast killed for him the fatted
calf. 31 And he said unto him, Son, thou art ever with me, and all
that I have is thine. 32 It was meet that we should make merry,
and be glad: for this thy brother was dead, and is alive again; and
was lost, and is found.*

God wants us to look to Him for our help and comfort, to be
our rod and staff, and to put Him first in our lives. He knows the
trials and tribulations that are to be suffered on this earth so He
gave Jesus Christ to the world to show us the way to live in peace
and security. Why not take advantage of such a wonderful
opportunity?

As we seek His Presence in the Silence, we are made aware
that the Kingdom of Heaven is within. "In all thy ways,
acknowledge Him and He shall direct thy paths" (Proverbs 3:6
KJV).

With this acknowledgment and understanding of God as the
source of all our needs, our lives change. An all-knowing is
experienced and a peace will come over us with an understanding
that everything is good. Sometimes it is necessary to wait for the
inner guidance to show the way, this is where faith will sustain us.
At other times, we will find that the problem is solving itself and is
just fading away.

Jesus said that all we need is a little faith, like that of a grain of
mustard seed. I realize the difficulty in acquiring a real faith, and

in the beginning it may be blind faith. Remember when Jesus came down from the mountain and the father of a young boy who was possessed of the demon asked Him to heal his son? Jesus said, "Everything is possible to the man who believes" and the father responded, "I do believe, help me to believe more." (Mark 9:23, 24 Phillips). After the healing, the disciples asked Jesus why they had not been able to heal the boy themselves. Jesus replied, "Nothing can drive out this kind of thing except prayer" (Mark 9:29 Phillips).

Not enough can be said concerning belief as we practice the art of prayer for where there is doubt and fear, prayers are not answered. This is the working of spiritual law. Someone said to me, "I gave my problems to God last night, but I took them back this morning." Is this not true of human nature? We tend to think that we can do it all by ourselves. With the experience of the power of prayer just one time, life can never be the same again. That something that transcends the five physical senses becomes a reality. Whether the problems are small or large, it matters not, our Heavenly Father is waiting for us to release our lives to Him in full faith.

James Allan's book, *As a Man Thinketh*, has been a real source of inspiration to me. In this book the author speaks of the power of thought; it is another spiritual law. Thoughts are things, and thoughts are a form of prayer. To visualize the need as we pray is paramount to its becoming reality. It lends power to the prayer to visualize the one for whom we are praying in the happiness and health that God wills for them. Positive prayers bring positive answers. Negative prayers bring the same results as prayer minus faith. When there is a need to be met, do not discuss the problem with God, rather, just release it. Nothing else is necessary and to dwell on the negative aspects of the problem will reap negative results.

It has happened many times that pain has increased as a result of one person, in a state of anxiety and fear, praying and thinking of the one for whom they are praying as sick rather than well and happy as God intended. Another excellent book on the subject of the power of thought is Frank C. Laubach's *Prayer: The Mightiest Force in the World.*

If we try and do not receive an answer, then we have prayed amiss. It only takes the acknowledgment that the Kingdom of God is within. Learning to pray effectively is not easy, but it is simple, and with a grain of faith and daily practice, success is assured. With the first experience of answered prayer, faith leaps and fear is gradually replaced with inner security and peace. In John 10:10 Jesus said, "I am come that they might have life, and have it more abundantly" (KJV). Life will be more abundant through a sincere desire and effort to commune with God in prayer and meditation.

We must ask in order to receive, seek that we may find, and knock that the door or way may be opened to us. I have been extremely blessed as I have had many prayers answered in my life; but before my quest began I only prayed for help in extreme situations. However, my first experience of the power of prayer was during my husband's illness. He had a fatal kidney disease which ultimately resulted in a kidney transplant from his identical twin brother.

When I was told that Bob would not live, I literally tell apart. Our son was four years old and our baby daughter was six months of age. I wondered what I was going to do. I had never known such despair, fear and helplessness. This, even though I had been a Christian all my life. That meant nothing to me then; I had no foundation of faith to lean upon.

I was guided into a fuller understanding of God's love and how His love could become a reality through the help of my pastor, Dr. T. Cecil Myers, then of Grace United Methodist Church in Atlanta. He encouraged me to completely surrender this problem to God and told me that His tender love and mercy would take care of everything. With the realization that I could not handle this crisis by myself, I was able to surrender it all to Him and I did find that His grace was sufficient. This was whole new experience for me; I could not believe, it. Without this first experience with God I might never have found the Way.

As I felt His peace come over me and with the knowledge that everything would be alright, I experienced a sense of peace for the very first time. He never said, but I think that Dr. Myers was as surprised as I at this miraculous happening since he later wrote of this experience in the Atlanta Journal, calling it, "The Miracle of Prayer."

Then things began to fall into, place. My husband's twin brother, Ralph, offered one of his kidneys and Bob and Ralph left for Peter Bent Brigham Hospital in Boston where kidney transplants were first researched. Their operation was the twelfth of its kind in the world. As I arrived just prior to surgery and spoke with Bob, we both felt the power and the Presence of God that neither of us had ever known before. The Presence was with me during the six hours of surgery. It was the result, I believe, of the power of intercessory prayer as our friends in Atlanta prayed around the clock during the crucial twenty-four hours following surgery.

Prayer and meditation together. Prayer without entering the silence is incomplete prayer. How are we going to hear the answer if we are not still? It is only in the Silence that thoughts from God can enter. It is through meditation that we are made spiritually aware. Answered prayer and Divine guidance are synonymous; "Be still, and know that I am God" (Psalms 46:10 KJV).

God answers prayer in very subtle ways. There are not any ringing bells and clanging cymbals, but there is an inner knowledge of what to do. A thought just pops into mind, an unusual set of circumstances is created out of nowhere; sometimes when we least expect it, He goes before us to make the crooked places straight. These are some of the ways God answers prayer. God speaks from His Spirit to our spirit.

We must find and maintain a proper mental, physical and spiritual balance. Then we become whole persons and experience the fullness of life through effective prayer and meditation.

4 BE STILL... AND KNOW

"Meditate upon these things; give thyself wholly to them; that thy profiting may appear to all"

1 Timothy 4:15 KJV

Meditation, or entering the Silence, is the key to finding the Inner Self, the God within. This is entering the Kingdom of Heaven within, and being born again into a new life.

It has been through the daily practice of prayer and meditation that I have been able to move from the darkness into the Light. By coming into the realization of the real Inner Self, the divinity within, there has come a pure love of God and self which must come before true love of others can flow naturally. In Matthew 22:37, 38 Jesus said, "Thou shalt love the Lord thy God with all thy heart, and all thy soul and with all thy mind. This is the first and great commandment. And, there is a second like it: Thou shalt love thy neighbor as thyself. The whole of the Law and Prophets depends on these two commandments." (Phillips).

Meditation is absolutely the surest way to success in spiritual development. This is the process that opens the soul to the Spirit of God; it is an experience of inner illumination and the attainment of Christ consciousness. Paul was speaking of this when he said, "Let the mind be in you, which was also in Christ Jesus" (Philippians 2:5 KJV).

Spiritual development through meditation is of vast importance. Actually, it is just as important as the nourishment we take for our physical bodies. Most people are unaware of this and do not realize that this is the way to inner peace and the answer to inner turmoil. We must move from an intellectual concept to an actual inner experience with God. Religion, in order to become a vital force in man, must of necessity leave the realm of the intellect and enter the heart of man. Otherwise, when crises come the "theory of faith" is only an empty theory.

Through meditation, Christ within comes alive and personal divinity becomes a reality. Meditation takes God out of empty theory and symbology and into an active, creative force in life. Meditation allows a personal encounter with God. With John Wesley's "heart warming" experience at Aldersgate, his life was changed. Intellectually, he had already accepted Jesus as his personal Savior but his ministry was most ineffective, He was a wretched soul until he had this inner personal experience with Christ and was born again with this spiritual awakening.

Several years ago, on first hearing the "God is dead" theory espoused, it was difficult for me to understand how this idea could be conceived by men of theological training. Now I understand that for anyone God can indeed be dead if a personal encounter with His Christ Spirit within is never experienced. To live only on two levels, the mental and physical, is to live an unbalanced life. The soul sleeps and must be awakened to know the fullness of life and to live in perfect harmony and balance.

To enter the Silence is to enter a whole new dimension, as it is only in the Silence that the "still, small voice" of God can be heard. It is a known fact that more is learned by listening than by talking and prayer life is no exception. Yet, there is too much talking, with no time set aside for listening, in the average person's prayer life. It is only in the Stillness that an awareness of the omnipresence of God can be experienced as a mystical union within.

Being still and listening is acknowledging His Presence within, allowing Him to give answer to prayer requests, and experiencing inner growth. Prayer without the silent time would be like preparing a meal and never serving it. The power of prayer often comes in the Silence when answers are received and a personal encounter with God within becomes a reality.

In the meditative silence, spiritual awareness is increased and the spiritual nature developed. As this is accomplished, the result is a balance between the mental, physical, and spiritual selves. This is healing and wholeness as the total personality becomes integrated into one. Such was the message in the ministry of Jesus as His healings brought wholeness to fragmented lives then just as it does today.

I was privileged to hear Dr. Oral Roberts speak to a group of ministers at Emory University recently. He stated that in order to become whole persons as God intended, a reverse in the order of our lives must be made. Many live on an intellectual plane with the spirit subjugated or squelched completely. The mind must be made into an instrument of spirit. The mind or intellect should carry out the guidance received on the spiritual level. This reverse order is necessary before wholeness and an integrated life can be accomplished. Dr. Roberts gave as an example Adam in the immortal, pure spiritual state before he ate from the tree of knowledge, thereby becoming mortal man.

As spiritual beings we are immortal and when the Christ within, or the Christ consciousness, is awakened, the truth that we do live, move, and have our being in God, who dwells within as the Christ Spirit becomes a total reality. This is immortality right here on earth; it is entering the Kingdom in which the mind of Christ within functions through the human mind.

Jesus said to go into our closets to pray and be alone with God. By closet He meant to draw within, for here is where God dwells. If time is not taken to be alone with God in meditation and prayer, we can become frayed, frustrated, drained,. and weary. If this happens then illness often follows. All of this can be prevented by understanding the physical and emotional need for this communion and then meeting this need through meditation.

It is through daily seeking God within that we discover negative attitudes that block us from God and prevent His Spirit from having full sway in our lives. Once there is an awareness of these negative emotions, then it is much easier to make the necessary corrections toward wholeness and health.

The Kingdom of Heaven is entered through the Silence of meditation. In most instances this is a gradual process and to the degree that the Kingdom is entered is the degree that living under Grace is realized. In John 13:36 Jesus said, "My Kingdom is not of this world." (KJV). It was difficult for the disciples to understand what He meant by this, and this is still true for many today. It is so very important to understand that the Kingdom can be now and not sometime after physical death. The spiritual progress to be made in the spiritual world is dependent on the spiritual development made here and now in this phase of life.

To live under Grace is the crucifixion of ego or self will: and the resurrection of the Christ within. It is surrendering self will to live completely within His will. This certainly is not easy to achieve but, the rewards of inner peace, harmony within the environment, and full faith to meet every situation of life are worth every minute spent in this endeavor.

Jesus often went off to be alone with God, renewing Himself by gaining sustenance from the Source of all manna. He would go to the mountains or into the wilderness to contemplate, meditate, and pray that His soul might be restored. After these times away, He was able to minister to the needs of man.

Today, as people swarm to the beaches, campsites, and mountains, it is for the purpose of restoring their souls. This may not be realized on a conscious level but is a very real inner need satisfied by getting away to find peace and quiet. How many times have we all done this? The restoring qualities received around water made the beach my favorite place to be as a teenager and it still is today.

In our world today we live such a harried, rush-rush existence, always trying to solve life's problems through our human abilities. It is little wonder that many needlessly suffer unhappy, frustrated, and discontented lives constantly plagued by illness. God's will for each and every one of us is the wholeness and health which make for inner peace and joy. He offers the peace that passes understanding, but this cannot be found to any lasting satisfaction through the physical intellect. Any lasting peace of mind can only be found within, through our spirit communicating with God's Spirit. It has been in meditation that I have found a personal relationship with God through His Spirit in Christ within me. Anyone can have this same kind of relationship by beginning the daily practice of meditation today.

Here are a few instructions in meditation that should help the beginner. These should be done every day at the same time and place if possible, starting with fifteen minutes and working up to thirty minutes or more.

Find a quiet place and sit in a straight chair or lie down flat; the point is that the spine must be straight. In the beginning the student may tend to go to sleep, for this reason I suggest sitting.

Sit with the spine straight, feet flat on the floor and hands laying loosely in the lap. Shrug the shoulders to loosen and relax these muscles. Let your entire body go completely limp. Feel the tension flow from your body and out through the toes.

Beginning with your head in the center position, eyes closed, go through the following movements three times each; be very gentle as the neck muscles may be very stiff at first.

1. From center position, chin to chest and back to center (three times).

2. From center position, head backward as far as possible (three times).

3. From center to right shoulder (three times).

4. From center to left shoulder (three times).

5. Rotate head counterclockwise (three times).

6. Rotate head clockwise (three times).

These exercises are tremendously important, as the neck and head are areas that build the most tension in the body. The purpose of these exercises is to bring total relaxation to the body so that there is no awareness of the physical body. As this is accomplished, inner spiritual awareness increases.

Another exercise which is very important for total relaxation is breathing. Breathe deeply three times; this will cleanse the lungs of all stale air and fill them with fresh oxygen. This is energizing and healing. Take in a deep breathe through the nostrils. Hold it to the count of seven, exhale through the mouth until the abdomen is completely flat. Do this three times.

Now let the breathing flow rhythmically. With eyes closed focus your vision on the forehead or third eye. Imagine a screen and see the words, "Be still . . . and know . . . God." Hold this affirmation in your mind's eye until the mind is quiet and there is no awareness of the body. Feel complete relaxation and peace flow throughout the body. The mind is now much more alert and aware, more open and receptive. This is the Silence where God is, it is entering the Holy of Holies.

With the eyes completely relaxed and closed you may become aware of light. You may find words or knowledge coming in, and you will recognize it as Truth. At this time ask Christ whatever you will and in the Silence wait upon Him and He will heal every care.

Any affirmation that brings the knowledge of God closer should be used, such as "Be still and know God." The purpose is to increase the awareness of the Spirit within while decreasing the awareness of the physical body and quieting the human consciousness.

If thoughts keep rushing in, recreate the affirmation and start over. It is often very difficult at first to quiet the mind; we are just not accustomed in this society to ever being still and quiet except when asleep. Meditation is accumulative; that which is achieved is never lost. It is like attempting anything new - a musical instrument or a physical sport - it only takes practice and patience. It is not something that can be pushed and it slows down the process to strain and try too hard. Do not be discouraged; keep practicing once every day and eventually success will come. In time, God will be experienced in the most glorious and rapturous ecstasy the mind can comprehend.

There are countless benefits to the daily practice of meditation, and often there is a life transformation as God is experienced within and a real, understanding of self is established. The understanding of the purpose for life is one of the greatest assets of meditation. So few people ever know that there is a divine purpose for their lives; that there is a Divine order to the universe that includes mankind. Many people have not planned beyond the employment years and therefore have never found their niche - the real purpose for their lives.

Unless a higher purpose for life is discovered, life becomes a routine of getting up, going to work, coming home, and going to bed - an endless round of nothingness. For example, there are many people who never find the right occupation - that challenging job where potential may be reached and satisfaction with a job well done is experienced.

This type situation is not necessary when it is realized that through seeking answers for life situations within ourselves, meaning and purpose can be found. Without that seeking within through meditation, it is certain that I would never have found the Divine purpose for my life. There would be no healing work, lectures, or any of the many things I now enjoy so very much.

When our children were small, I would wonder, "What in the world would I do when they grow up and leave home?" That will be happening next year when our son goes off to college and thank God we have found meaning and purpose beyond raising our children.

Medical doctors are beginning to use meditation in the treatment of cancer and heart disease. Dr. Carl Simonton, a radiotherapist from Fort Worth, Texas, has been very successful in healing cancer through meditation and group psychotherapy, along with conventional medical treatment. He began this method when he noticed that all of his cancer patients had one thing in common; they all had suffered some form of emotional stress several years before the onset of the disease. He felt the direct approach to the cause of the disease was the best way to treat the cancer. In other words, remove the emotional cause and the body will respond by getting well. He has the patient use the power of the mind to visualize the cancer cells being destroyed by the white cells. Meditation brings total relaxation to the body which aides healing as it removes tension and creates calmness in the mind.

Even if the deeper spiritual experience is never reached, meditation through total physical relaxation is fantastic for regeneration of the cells in healing. Tension and stress cause an imbalance in the body's metabolism and over an extended period of time can result in physical illness; therefore, it is easy to see how total relaxation through meditation could restore the body's chemistry to normal.

My own religious training started in the Cradle Roll of Bull Street Baptist Church in Savannah, Georgia. I had been an active church member all of my life and had always loved the Church, but I had never really comprehended what Church life was all about. I recall wondering at some point in my young adult life, if others actually felt God's love and did return that feeling as so many professed to do. Although I wanted this experience, it did not really seem possible; it seemed to be just a beautiful theory. In an intellectual way, I believed that God loved me, but there had been no actual personal experience that manifested this love realistically for me. Looking back, I now understand what was lacking in my religious life and the cause of this emptiness within me. It was my hungry soul crying out for fulfillment, the fulfillment that can only come through realization of His abiding Presence and communion with the Christ within. The fulfillment that comes from seeking His guidance, by listening and then knowing His will for every situation.

It has been through the daily practice of meditation that my life has changed and without which, I truly believe, I would still be back in my pit. I refer to my life before the spiritual path began, as the time when I was in a deep, black pit from which there seemed to be no escape. Every day was a trauma of fear. I would hang these fearful emotions on the first available posts not realizing that the fear actually was within me. My fears had no relation to that which I thought I feared. Even such things as my husband's safety going to and from work - the real fear was my own extreme insecurity. Hostility also was a major problem; and depression became an almost constant state of being.

It was at this time, when I felt that I could no longer cope, that I had two paranormal experiences that literally opened my eyes to the possibility that maybe, just maybe, there was something more to life than I previously had known.

The mother of my sister-in-law. and a very dear friend, told me that she had cancer and had about six months to live. One day, while visiting her in the hospital, I asked her a question that I had never spoken about to anyone before, but something that I had given a lot of thought to. I asked, "If it is possible to communicate from the spirit world, would you promise to try to communicate with me when you pass?" I was afraid that she would think that I was off my rocker but, so very lovingly she said. "Yes, my dear, I believe just as you do, and I promise that I will try to communicate with you." At this time in my life I had never read the first word concerning spirit communication or any of the paranormal subjects; my world then was very small.

She passed in November of that year and all during that first week I waited for - I knew not what. Nothing happened and the whole experience was forgotten, probably because I really did not believe that it could really happen.

Three weeks after she passed I was sitting on the floor of our living room wrapping Christmas presents when suddenly I was not alone; there was a Presence with me. I walked across to the den thinking someone had come in, but there was no one there. When I sat back down the Presence seemed closer and I was frightened. Then the realization hit me: "It's Mrs. Lord!" It is difficult to describe what I was experiencing at that moment, but I said to myself, "OK, kiddo, you asked for it. Now, do you want this?" The answer was "No, this frightens me," and with the completion of that thought the Presence was gone as quickly as it had come. Since that experience I have felt a telepathic communication with my parents and others and they have been experiences that I shall always cherish.

With this and another paranormal experience that will be described later, there was born within me a spark of hope. It is said, that when the student is ready the teacher appears; this certainly seemed to be true for as the desire to know more was created within me, the right books seemed to come along. This was the beginning of the spiritual path that has led to wholeness and a wonderful, new life.

After several years of seeking God through meditation and study, the depression and hostility within me had faded away, although I was not conscious of it at the time. This is the beauty of the transforming power of Christ through meditation. My husband, Bob, calls this my "metamorphosis." This is an excellent description since all my negative attitudes had been mysteriously replaced by a bright, positive outlook on life. A wellspring of hope that brought a lasting change surged through me. It was not a temporary remission of the old attitudes, nor was it a transient dream that would vanish and leave me once again in my pit.

The changes brought by meditation are gradual and subtle, but are sure and permanent. The most surprising change that occurred was my attitude concerning problems. Where once I hated problems and would lament, "I do not need any more problems," I now view problems as blessings. The first time that I said this was in a lecture and I nearly fainted when the words reached my ears - "Did I say that?" This is just how subtle the transformation within can be. Without adversity and problems there can be no growth. This is a positive and negative world so in order to know and appreciate happiness, it is necessary to go through the valley to reach the mountain top. Someone said, "The worst affliction is not to be afflicted." This is well said, for it is through pain and suffering that growth and maturity are achieved. As the popular Lynn Anderson song goes, "I never promised you a rose garden."

Meditation creates a positive attitude and negativity fades away. This is necessary to a harmonious environment. Man is the victim of his own thought process; whatever is thought becomes fact. Like attracts like, and negative thoughts attract negative consequences just as beautiful thoughts create positive results. Everything that was ever made had its birth in the form of a thought. As little as it is realized, man creates his own circumstances. Heaven or hell is created right here on earth by means of the thought process. It is useless to try to change our environment except by inner alteration. As attitudes change, then the outward circumstances are transformed. This is natural law in operation. "As you sow, so shall you reap." (Galatians 6:7 Phillips). It is really a miracle to see the attitudes of others change to warmth and love, and what had seemed like an impossible situation, suddenly healed. These are the marvelous reapings of a positive outlook and can happen to anyone through seeking to know self and to encounter God within in the meditative Silence.

As many changes were being wrought in my life, the most significant change came with the revelation that I had an ego problem. This revelation occurred during meditation in my prayer group one evening, I heard, as if someone had spoken within, "Your ego is holding you back." This was a complete shock to me. How could anyone who has spent the better part of their life feeling inferior have an ego problem? But it is just not possible to solve a problem until the problem is recognized. With the acceptance of this, as truth from Christ within, I was able to face the fact that my extreme desire to sing was motivated by ego.

Meditation had opened my soul to the truth, therefore my ego problem could be dealt with for as Jesus taught, knowing the truth results in freedom. I had taken voice lessons for several years, had been tested by the best voice teachers in Atlanta, and had been told that I had great potential if I really worked at it every day. Nothing ran smoothly during this time, but never once did I question why. I was determined to sing, and that was that. In the prayer group, we talked about the fact that one way we can know God's will, rather than our own, is that everything runs smoothly when it is His will. At that time, I really prided myself that I was living within God's will, but upon examining the truth of why singing was so very important, I became aware that my singing certainly was not to God's glory, but rather to my own. This was a very painful thing to accept, but with the release of this self will, I found a peace and freedom that I had never before known.

This one selfish desire had blocked me from seeing the Divine purpose for my life. With a deep desire to find His Divine purpose, I was finally able to surrender the singing desire and, again surrender my life to accept God's will each day. The same week, I received my first invitation to lecture. Then doors began opening for the healing ministry, although I was still unaware of the magnitude of my calling. It was no coincidence that these openings came, rather they were the result of the natural law of cause and effect.

To be born again is not a one-time proposition, but rather many rebirths as the negative barriers to God's love are removed one by one. It has been my experience that being born again, or experiencing healing of the soul is a gradual process as a oneness with God is sought.

Then one day we will look back on the panorama of this life with satisfaction... when Christ will say, "Well done my good and faithful servant."

5 THE STILL, SMALL VOICE

"See, I stand knocking at the door, If anyone listens to my voice
and opens the door, I will go   into his house and dine with him,
and he with me"

Revelations 3:20 Phillips

There seems to be a psychic revolution going on now with
much interest in ESP and the paranormal experiences. Among
youth especially there is a growing interest in phenomena beyond
the five physical senses. The Jesus Freak movement and the use of
drugs to affect an altered state of consciousness are evidence of
this interest among young people.

However, with all the interest in this fascinating subject there
apparently is very little understanding among many people. Most
think that they do not have any extrasensory perception that it is
a talent of only a privileged few. Then there are others who
vehemently deny that ESP exists at all, their theory being that it is
only the logical mind at work.

Psychic phenomena and the paranormal are familiar terms of our time which correlate with the miracles of Biblical times. There is no difference; only the terminology has been changed.

What the Church has traditionally called miracles, Paul wrote of as the "spiritual gifts." Psychic and spiritual gifts are the same; in the Greek translation psychic means soul, and all spiritual gifts come from God, the essence of our soul.

The early Church developed around the healings, visions, prophesies and miracles of its earliest missionaries as recounted in the Book of Acts. Miracles were not just experienced in the time of Jesus; they occur today but are referred to by different names. "Clairvoyance," a direct visual reception beyond the five senses, reflects the same phenomena as Jesus demonstrated with the Samaritan woman at the well in the Gospel of John: "Go and call your husband and then come back here," said Jesus to her. "I haven't got a husband!" the woman answered. "You are quite right in saying, 'I haven't got a husband'," replied Jesus, "for you have had five husbands and the man you have now is not your husband at all. Yes, you spoke the simple truth when you said that." John 4:16-18 (Phillips)

"Clairaudience" is a direct auditory reception whose Biblical example is found in Jesus' baptism when the people there heard, "Thou art my beloved Son;" (Luke 3:22 KJV).

"Prophecy" relates to the prediction of the future by intuitive means of which there are many examples in the Bible. Paul displayed this at the end of the Acts when he foretold the progress of his voyage to Rome. Jesus exhibited this when He said He would be betrayed thrice before the cock crowed. "Mysticism" relates to the type of inner experience of God experienced in

Isaiah 6 by Ezekiel, John's vision in Revelations, as well as countless other visions recounted in the Bible.

"Mediumship" relates Biblically to Jesus when he appeared with Moses and Elijah on the Mount of Transfiguration. "Telekinesis" relates to the power of thought as it affects physical change, as when Jesus changed the water into wine at Cana. "Apparition" is a dematerialization which Jesus demonstrated in appearances following His Resurrection. Healing is demonstrated by Jesus' ministry, as well as, by His disciples and the early missionaries of the New Testament.

In First Corinthians, Paul lists the spiritual gifts; this is exactly the same phenomena listed by scientists researching the psychic today. He wrote of the psychic or spiritual gifts because of the misuse of these gifts at Corinth. Paul, one of the greatest psychics, relates in First Corinthians the place for the spiritual gifts in the Church. Paul says that the spiritual or psychic gifts are a part of the whole Church, but are secondary to faith for without faith all else is worthless; he also says that love is the foundation which will last when all other things pass away.

Paranormal experience abound not only in the New Testament, but the Old Testament is a chronology of prophecies, visions, and other unseen powers. Joseph was known for his talent to interpret dreams, and this ability led to his becoming second in command to the Pharaoh in Egypt. There was Deborah, a prophetess who used her intuitive powers to guide Barak, the Hebrew captain, in his victory over the Canaanite commander, Sisera. She also precognized Sisera's death at the hands of a woman. It was through Samuel that the precognitive impression of David's role was given, and afterward the chore of anointing him to be Saul's replacement.

Spiritual gifts are a significant part of the Christian Church for the Church focuses its purpose on the life and teachings of Jesus. Jesus practiced all of the spiritual gifts and told us in John 14:12 (Phillips), "I assure you that the man who believes in me will do the same things that I have done, yes, and he will do even greater things than these, for I am going away to the Father. Whatever you ask the Father in my name, I will do - that the Son may bring glory to the Father. And if you ask me anything in my name, I will grant it."

Jesus gave the commission to His disciples and the Church to go out and teach, preach, and heal. He is saying in the Gospel of John that it is possible that the works that He did, those who believe in Him also could do.

It is so vitally important that the Christian Church be attuned to the times in this psychic revolution. The growing interest in the paranormal is a direct result of hungry souls seeking nourishment. The Church is the natural place for the soul to be fed. Miracles are a part of our Christian heritage and if the need for this is not met there, then people will go where it can be found. Here it is dangerous, for there are certainly many charlatans and frauds ready and willing to take over where the Church leaves off. In the church school class that I teach, a gentleman recently said, concerning the paranormal, that he had believed in supernatural happenings but was afraid to talk about them in the Church. In working with church groups, I have heard this many times, and my experience has been that there is as much interest, perhaps more, among active church members as that among those who have left the Church.

There are three major purposes for the spiritual gifts that are as practical for this age as they were in Biblical times. These experiences should be used for acknowledging and glorifying God, for personal protection, and for helping others.

Jesus said that He had to go to the Father that we might have the Comforter, the Holy Spirit. It is through the Holy Spirit that the spiritual gifts are made manifest. We are given intuition for guidance and protection and these flashes should be heeded; not disregarded as coincidence, vague hunches, or imagination. There is no way to prove this, but I honestly believe that in every case of accident and tragedy that someone involved had a premonition but ignored it, or was unaware of the inner warning. This is one major reason why developing spiritual awareness is so very important. God provided us with this built in protection, and it is important to discern when Spirit speaks. How wonderful it would be if this were taught in Church schools.

The foremost part of Jesus' ministry was healing; He stated that through healing, men might know God's love and glorify Him. Healing can be the beginning of a sincere spiritual life, as men's eyes are opened to the truth of Gods healing love forgiving nature. There is no more awesome experience than to see another healed through a human channel. Healing, more than any other gift, manifests the majesty, wonder, and mystery of the Infinite love and power of God.

Spiritual gifts should not be sought for they are just what the Word states, they are gifts given when we are God centered in our motivation. When the student is seriously seeking a personal encounter with God, then the spiritual gifts may be given. There is danger in pursuing psychic phenomena as the reasons are often for personal gain, power, or for parlor games. It is possible to be psychic and not spiritual, but the gifts are always apparent in the spiritually developed person.

The non-physical world is as much a part of this life as the physical world, and an understanding of these mysteries will add tremendously to this dimension of living and the majesty of God into greater reality. Each time any of the spiritual gifts are experienced, it is a manifestation of God, and should never be ridiculed, scorned, or criticized because of a lack of understanding from one who has never had a spiritual experience. But rather the witnessing or experiencing of the spiritual gifts should increase the awareness of the magnitude of God and the desire for a deeper religious life.

It is through meditation that the preparation is made to receive the gifts of the Spirit. Man's potential for spiritual growth is unlimited, and as wholeness is materialized, it is then possible for all the gifts to be expressed. It has been thought that only one gift could be received but this is a mistake, for the degree that wholeness is achieved and the Kingdom entered, all that the Father has is ours.

Having been intuitive all of my life, I assumed that everyone had this same ability. However, following two rather unusual paranormal experiences, I became aware that paranormal occurrences were not that common. In his book, *The Power of Perception*, Dr. Marcus Bach calls such phenomena the "commonly unfelt." The commonly unfelt is any sensing beyond the five senses of touch, taste, smell, hearing, and sight.

Some years ago two unusual paranormal experiences served to be a catalyst for my spiritual quest. While in the throes of cleaning the house for the Christmas ho1idays I had an immediate feeling that the decorator towels that were to be washed would be lost. This made no sense at all as nothing had ever been taken from the Laundromat where our clothes were dried each week. An argument ensued for several minutes between my human consciousness and this inner guidance. My human consciousness won because anything else seemed to be utter foolishness. Upon returning to pick up the clothes, sure enough, the towels were gone. Certainly this may seem trivial and mundane to some, since the towels could be replaced, but the message it brought to me, along with the other paranormal experience shared in the preceding chapter, was the beginning of a whole new adventure in that spiritual quest that led to a complete transformation of my life.

These phenomena happened within a week of each other, and could not be mistaken for coincidence. These were answers to a prayer for the help needed to bring me out of the depths of despair and hopelessness where I had been lodged for so long. This was God literally knocking at my door, the door of my consciousness. God is constantly working to gain the attention of each of His children, and apparently, this is what it took to get my attention.

This experience is a case of not following the intuition and yet gaining from the experience. Had I followed the guidance and not taken the towels, I may have remained in that hopeless pit; instead, it led to freedom, and a life of purpose and fulfillment. This is a paradox for certainly we are to depend on inner guidance. God used a mundane situation to bring a much needed message with no significant loss.

Recently, following a lecture on psychic phenomena as it relates to the spiritual life, a lady said to me, 'I had no idea that ESP had any relationship to God." She has summarized in that statement the limited understanding of the paranormal held by the majority of the public.

Prayer, which everyone at one time or another turns to, is an extrasensory experience. Prayer is communicating with God, and unseen Spirit. This is spirit-to-Spirit communication when practiced correctly, and is thus an extrasensory experience.

Our world is a perilous one in which we are met with many dangers and pitfalls, but our loving Divine Creator has provided protection against these problems through the power of extrasensory perception. The answer to every problem, and the solution of all dilemmas can be found within through awareness of the still, small voice. This is the way that God has provided for our guidance and protection. It is through being attuned to the Christ within that awareness of His will is made known.

One of the first experiences that I had in helping another was through a clairvoyant vision involved the loss of the main door keys to the home of a friend. Upon meditating on the lost key, I was given the knowledge through a vision that a young girl, whom I had never seen before, had the key. When I related this information to our friend, she recognized this girl to be her daughter's best friend. Upon investigation, it was learned that this friend had taken the key in order to use their home during the family's absence on vacation. With this knowledge the problem was solved and new locks were not necessary, saving our friend a great deal of expense.

By being aware of this built-in protection through inner guidance, and then following this guidance, disaster can be avoided. This has been my experience on several different occasions. One such incident involved an invitation to accompany a friend on a trip out of town. One Sunday afternoon she called to ask me to go with her to Chattanooga, Tennessee for a few days. Immediately, there was within me a sense of foreboding, and the feeling that I was not to take this trip. On the way out of town, my friend came by to ask me again to go with her and as she left, she said, "You know, I really do not want to go for some reason.' This, I believe, was her inner guidance though she was not fully aware of this, probably because of the business responsibility involved in the trip.

Halfway to her destination, she was involved in a terrible automobile accident that almost took her life. It is very likely that it would have taken mine as the other car hit hers on the passenger side. I have wondered so many times why my warning could not have been more explicit so that I might have warned my friend. Perhaps it would not have been so had I been more aware than I was at that time in my life.

Our safety and security, to a great extent, are dependent on the awareness of this inner guidance. It is God's will that we be protected from the dangers of this uncertain world. Man's free will is often the author of many tragedies, but as spiritual development is accomplished, man's free will is brought into harmony with God's will and Divine protection is manifested.

Dreams, God's Forgotten Language, by John Sanford, is a very descriptive book. The significance of dreaming is not generally understood except in the area of psychiatry and psychic research, but it is a Divine instrument, available to everyone. Dreams may or may not be remembered, but everyone dreams and memory of the dream life can be cultivated.

Dreams are very much a part of the Bible, both Old and New Testament, and should be an instrument for guidance in everyday life.

There are several levels of dreaming with very definite

psychological meanings, one of which comes from the higher self to give counsel and guidance for personal growth and for situational problems. This type of dream will usually awaken the dreamer, and this is one way of determining that this is a significant dream message. These dreams should be written down and studied for the proper meaning as they are created in symbology and therefore must be interpreted in order to comprehend the full meaning of the dreams.

The purpose for precognitive knowledge or warnings in dreams or otherwise is that the circumstances may be altered through prayer or by physical intervention, depending upon the need.

Several years ago our son was playing high school football and his leg was broken during afternoon practice. He had dreamed the night before that he had broken his leg with the actual occurrence being exactly the same as the dream message. However, he did not remember the dream in time to prevent the accident. He remembered it as he was running down the football field, which was a little late!

Editor's Note: *Breaking my leg was itself an answer to a prayer. My best friend talked me into playing football because he said the girls at school would be more interested in dating me if I were on the team. I quickly found that I hated football, but I wouldn't quit because I feared the ridicule of my peers for being a quitter. I prayed for an honorable way to leave the team. Unfortunately, I got what I asked for.*

Remembering dreams can be cultivated, and should be for they are a very real source of protection as well as guidance. The best technique for remembering dreams is simply by programming oneself to remember. This can be mastered by telling yourself that the dream will be remembered upon awakening. This should be done just before going to sleep, and a note pad and pencil kept by the bed so that the dream may be jotted down on awakening.

"Let me sleep on it" is a very common expression with a very literal meaning; for when the conscious mind is at rest, it is more receptive to inner truth. When decisions are made based on inner guidance, be assured that it is the right decision.

Another area where there seems to be little understanding is that of astral projection or out-of- body experiences. This is a perfectly normal phenomena that occurs with everyone, remembered or not. Psychiatry refers to this experience as dissociation.

This usually occurs at sleep when a dream seems so real that it is thought to have actually happened; this very probably was an astral projection. Out-of-body occurrences are fairly common during surgery, child birth, and severe illness when the spirit or etheric body leaves the physical body. Often these experiences are remembered and the patient is able to relate observing the surgery, or the birth of the baby as a bystander and not as a participant.

This can be very frightening if it is not understood, and in most cases the first remembered experience is frightening. When my husband was ill with kidney disease, he found himself looking down on his body in the bed and immediately thought that he had died. Even though he knew that he had a fatal illness and might not live, this was still a very frightening experience as it was the first time that he was conscious of ever being out of his body.

For this reason, it is very important that the public be educated on this subject so that there will be an understanding that astral projection is a normal occurrence, and not to be feared.

Actually, it is freedom for the spirit, and also a time for learning on a subconscious level. Mystical experiences can occur on this level as Paul states in II Corinthians 12:3 (KJV), "And I know such a man, (whether in the body, or out of the body, I cannot tell: God knoweth)."

Another beauty of this phenomena is that it is proof that there is a spiritual body, and therefore continuing life after death of the physical body. For the one who is skeptical concerning life after death, just one out-of-body experience will erase all doubt. Surprisingly, there are many Christians who have trouble believing that there really is life after death. An excellent reference on this subject is *Life Begins At Death* by Leslie Weatherhead.

There is much wonder and beauty in extrasensory experiences as they bring a deeper reality of God and the vastness of His Universe. Adjectives such as wonder, awe, majesty, and glory are used to try to describe the indescribable sensing of God.

It is my understanding that all but one of our astronauts went into some form of spiritual or psychic work following their space trips, having experienced firsthand the majesty of our Heavenly Father and Divine Creator.

A study of the paranormal can be very fulfilling as it brings an understanding of natural law and strengthens faith in the Eternal God.

6 THE GIFT OF HEALING

"Behold thou art made whole..."

John 5:14 KJV

After several years in my spiritual quest had passed, I felt that my life was changing. Through daily meditation and prayer, and through the study and fellowship of a small prayer group, many inner problems and emotional hang-ups had been resolved. I had literally come alive and was vibrant and excited about life. I had never known that I could be excited about anything. My pastor had once asked me, "What excites you?" and my reply was that I did not know, that nothing really excited me at all. Now it is completely different; life is exciting, and everyday a marvelous adventure. Certainly there are still those low moments, but I believe these are the natural positive and negative forces of life. The lows are not too low and the highs are not too high. This is the balance I have referred to which constitutes wholeness and fulfillment. This is what spiritual awareness can do for everyone. It will open the mind to the truth and the truth will be the source of freedom from the shackles of negative emotions that block personal potential, the joy of fulfillment, and thus the experience of wholeness.

It was during this time that I was physically healed of a chronic condition. On awakening one morning, I experienced a clairvoyant recall of an apparent dream. In the vision I was given the sense that a lesion, which had been producing rather serious symptoms, could be healed through prayer.

I, of myself, would never have thought to pray for my own healing, or for anyone's healing as such. Certainly I believed in the power of prayer and the many tremendous examples of answered prayer, but healing, that was different! Yet, as I pondered this unusual happening, it seemed to make sense. When Bob had the kidney disease I had prayed for him although I did not know exactly what I was praying for - only that I desperately wanted him to live. God certainly had worked a miracle there. Well, I knew nothing about spiritual healing, but I prayed for my own healing in the full belief that I would be healed. The next morning the symptoms were gone and have never reoccurred. That was six years ago; what a fantastic introduction to spiritual healing!

The healing process is as complex as the reasons for sickness and disease. It is my understanding that the majority of physical illness is psychosomatic in origin. A person becomes physically ill when the human mind is in conflict with the soul; or as the theologian might say, "There is a tug of war between the flesh and the spirit."

Hate, selfishness, hostility, resentment, fear and pride are the culprits that cause physical and emotional il1ness. These, I believe, are sins as it is these negative emotions that block us from God's love, guidance, wholeness, and health. It is easy to understand how emotions affect the body as in the case of sudden fear - the body responds with weakness and trembling, or as in the case of extreme joy - the eyes fill with tears of happiness.

Then how much more can negative emotions, carried within over a long period of time, cause physical illness? This is spiritual law in operation. Since the real self is spirit, when the soul or spirit is in conflict with the human will, it is manifested physically as illness and disease.

Spiritual healing and development cannot be separated for as we develop our inner awareness, we are being spiritually healed. This is what spiritual growth is all about. It is through this process that we become aware of negative emotions and can cast them out. This is the growth in Spirit and in Truth which results in our becoming a new person. As we bring about a balance in mind, body, and spirit, we become a whole, integrated personality. This is healing within and the birth of the inner spiritual person.

It is at this time in our development that the gifts of the Spirit may be received. When we seek God with our heart, mind, and soul, then the Holy Spirit is allowed to manifest itself as a particular gift. In my case, I was given the gift of healing. However, one should not seek spiritual gifts, but rather seek a oneness with God; the gifts will then be given.

Before we can give of ourselves, we first must prepare by searching within. Inner security is found by removing the negatives that are blocking progress. This is the healing of self which must come before the gifts of the Spirit and before true loving service can be successfully accomplished. As inner awareness and sensitivity increase, the capacity to love increases. This is one of the wonderful results of spiritual development.

Almost everyone whom I see for spiritual counseling and healing expresses a sincere desire to help others. This is the natural desire of the Christian heart and it is this same desire that makes inner illumination and healing possible.

Illness is the result of disobedience to God's will. All illness is contrary to God's divine purpose. God's will for all His children is absolute wholeness and health. If we refuse to follow His will and insist on pursuing our own selfish desires, then this is an open invitation to sickness and suffering. Whenever we begin to wonder why everything is going wrong, this is the reason.

When we put our trust in God and follow His direction, all is harmonious. When we follow our own desire and direction, life may go well, but it may not. In the material world, there is no guarantee of health, wealth, and happiness. It is only through living within His will that we overcome adversity to any degree and it is through this same adversity that we experience our greatest growth. Illness may be a good in our lives even though we tend to think of illness as an enemy. Illness can be beneficial if this time is used in reevaluation, and if it is realized that illness is a result of an inner conflict between the soul and the human personality. This should be a time of reflection, of soul searching, and of repentance (a turning around). Attitudes and emotions must change before healing and wholeness can be fully established. A problem cannot be solved until it is recognized, and this certainly includes an understanding of the reasons for illness.

Even with the common cold, when the emotions of the previous day are reviewed, we will very likely discover that the feeling of fear or loss experienced that day caused the cold. When that cause is realized and faced, the cold will then disappear. So it is with more serious maladies; when critically examined, our emotional state and our illnesses are inseparable.

It is the purpose of spiritual healing to remove the cause of illness. When the source of the disease in eliminated, the body responds by getting well and healthy again. Spiritual healing, spiritual counseling (which aids the patient in understanding how healing works), and meditation are the tools that help to bring wholeness and health to the ill individual.

The medical profession for the most part, treats the effect and not the cause illness; this will never bring about a permanent cure. If the cause is not removed, the patient will very likely become ill once again. However, both the medical profession and the clergy are working together more than ever to affect a wholeness that will help the individual to stay well, There are several resources on this subject that I highly recommend Morton Kelsey's, *Healing and Christianity* (an excellent resource for ministers); *The Will to Live*, by Arnold A. Hutschnecker, M.D.; and *Prayer Can Change Your Life*, by William R. Parker, Ph.D. These are very helpful in understanding the emotional demons that cause physical illness.

Love is the key to healing and to the degree that we love others is the degree that God can use us for His healing channel. Paul said that, "Love knows no limit to its endurance, no end to its trust, no fading of its hope; it can outlast anything. It is, in fact, the one thing that still stands when all else has fallen." (I Cor. 13:13 Phillips). Everyone, I believe, has the potential to be a healer; as we are all made in the image and likeness of God. However, I question that one can become an effective healer by simply studying and practicing healing techniques, even though it is possible to learn the various healing methods and to acquire an understanding of the principles of healing through a study course or workshop.

There are several techniques of healing, and therefore, there are different types of healers. Laying-on-hands is the most common technique of healing, and is a part of our Christian heritage. Jesus healed through touch, or even being touched, and it is one of the sacraments in the Christian Church. However, for the most part, laying-on-hands is ignored by the traditional church today.

Laying-on-hands is very much like the jumper cable that is used to revive a weak automobile battery. The battery is not dead; it just needs a charge. The same is true when we are sick. Energy is at a low level during illness and laying-on-hands increases this vital flow or energy. We live, move, and have our being in God. God is energy. He uses the physical body as a channel or "jumper cable" through which His healing energy may flow to restore and heal the sick.

Healing is a part of spiritual law and it is present within everyone. However, when negative attitudes, physical illness or accident prevail, it is often necessary to restore the body's vital energy through natural healing power - through laying-on-hands.

Healing is a very complex subject, and one not to be taken lightly especially when it is thought that this is the very direction our life is taking. I do not recommend that anyone seek to be a healer and I agree with Joel Goldsmith, an author and authority in this field, that a healing ministry should be avoided unless the call is so strong and certain that there is no alternative. There are numerous reasons for this. In order to be an effective healer, total commitment, discipline, and dedication is required. One must literally be in this world but not of it to the limit that it is possible for the consciousness to transcend the human level. This requires years of preparation and commitment through meditation and prayer.

It is necessary to guard against the negativity of others, including the news media, as this may affect the channeling of healing and render it ineffective.

Another factor is the public scorn and ridicule surrounding the field of healing today. Sometimes friendships may be lost due to a lack of understanding or ignorance, and embarrassment. Labels such as "nut" or "kook" or "witch" are not uncommon.

To some measure the healing ministry is a lonely life since so often one must walk alone. However, it is the most gratifying and fulfilling service that I could ever have undertaken. The knowledge that God has used even me to help to heal another is the most awesome experience of my life.

It was sometime before I became conscious that I was indeed being led into a healing ministry. I had shared with others in lectures and study groups the healings that had come through me, but I thought, that just affirming that Christ does heal today was the extent of my own ministry. I really began to understand what was happening in my life when a friend was dramatically healed through me.

It was immediately following this incident that I knew that healing was His will for my life. I was alone at home when I felt a glorious Presence surrounding me and I knew that I had been chosen for a healing ministry.

The mother of my son's best friend, had suffered a massive coronary and was not expected to live. After praying for her for several days I intuitively knew that I was to go to the hospital to lay-on-hands. I seemed to know that I would be able to see her even though only her immediate family were allowed to visit. God did go before me to make the crooked places straight. The nurse permitted me to see her for five minutes.

After leaving the hospital, I experienced an all-knowing feeling that she was going to be well. Excitement filled me as I waited for the official word that she was going to live. Within twenty- four hours, she was moved from coronary care to a regular hospital room and in six weeks she was able to return to her bowling team.

This was especially unusual in that instantaneous healing is very rare. An interesting side note is that although I did not tell her of the reason for my visit, later she said to me, "The night you came to see me was significant somehow." I consider this to be a confirmation that at some level of consciousness she was aware that something unusual had happened to her. The doctor was at a loss to explain her complete recovery.

There have been many healings since this dramatic incident, but I never know what will happen next.

Editor's Note: *My good friend, Tony, and his family moved a few years later to another state, and we lost touch with each other. A few years ago, Tony and I reconnected via telephone. After catching up for a few minutes, he said to me. "I'll never forget how your mother saved my mother's life." I said, "What are you talking about?" I had completely forgotten the incident. He reminded me how my mother had snuck in to see his mother; put her hands on his mother's chest and prayed. And, how, much to the doctor's dismay, she was well the very next day.*

Over a year ago, a lady called and stated that she had terminal cancer of the bone and had been given six months to live. She came several times for healing as she continued with her medical therapy. Nine months later, her doctor was unable to find x-ray evidence or clinical evidence of the tumors that had been evident over various parts of her body.

In most cases, healing is progressive like this and not instantaneous for as illness is progressive, so is the healing process.

The question is always raised, "Why are some healed and some are not?" Only God in His infinite wisdom knows why, but there are some factors that are relevant to an explanation of this question.

Jesus would say to those who came to Him for healing, "Do you want to be healed?" This is a very pertinent question. Medical doctors know the extreme importance of the will to live. Without that will, all the medical treatment available is rendered useless. This is also a major factor in spiritual healing.

There are two forces that control man: the will to live and the will toward self-destruction. The decision for one or the other is made on the subconscious level and the individual may not be aware of this decision on a conscious level. This is one important area where the healer may use intuition to great advantage and thereby be of greater benefit to the patient concerned.

An example of the will to live versus the will toward self-destruction is a thirty-four year old mother of four children who requested that I come to the hospital for healing. She had a malignant tumor involving her liver and her abdominal cavity was filled with fluid. This was an inoperable cancer and she was not expected to live.

The young woman had asked for healing through the influence of a close friend, but told me that she was tired and weary, and she just did not want to cope any longer. Her husband had died the year before, and her desire to join him proved to be irreversible.

Immediately following the healing in the hospital, there was marked improvement. The tumor and the liver decreased rapidly in size and the liver function studies were normal within a few weeks.

Four months later she passed away from a secondary infection of the lung. The interesting point here is that an autopsy showed a normal liver with scar tissue. There was no cancer visible to the eye, though there were a few microscopic cancer cells found in another part of her body.

Clearly, this is an example of the will toward self-destruction making the difference in her complete recovery.

Another factor influencing healing is belief. Jesus would say, after one of His many healings, "Thy faith hath made thee whole" (Matthew 9:22 KJV). Often I have observed that after someone calls for a healing appointment, when they arrive they are already much improved. This is spiritual law at work again. There was a decision and a commitment made to be healed, and this caused a release of the negative blockage of the vital life force inherent in everyone.

However, there are some who are healed that are very skeptical or who perhaps are unaware of the intercessory prayers being lifted for their healing. Herein lies the great mystery of our loving and divine Creator.

During a second visit to speak to a group of church women in Athens, Georgia, I learned of a healing that had taken place during my previous visit the year before. A woman there had been healed of very painful arthritic knees. She said the pain was so severe that a friend had to help her into and out of the car when they came for the meeting. It was only on returning home that she realized the pain was gone. When her friend said, "Your legs, what has happened to your legs? I did not have to help you into the car!" Her attendance at the meeting had been reluctant for she was skeptical of the whole spiritual field and especially of healing. She told me that as we were leaving that day, I had touched her shoulder and said, "I am especially glad you came today." I did not remember this, nor was I aware that she was healed, though I did feel a great charisma with her and spoke of her to my husband on our return home.

Intercessory prayer is vital in any healing ministry and is very effective when intercession is approached with a positive attitude.

A friend of mine had been troubled with a chronic bleeding ulcer for several years with talk of possible surgery. For a period of several weeks, I concentrated on healing prayer, visualizing him well and happy as God wills him to be. Several months later he told me that the ulcer had completely healed and had left no scar tissue. This is extremely unusual, for a chronic bleeding ulcer is very difficult to cure without surgery. In this case, my friend did not know of my prayers for his healing, but this had no effect on the power of prayer. It is the faith of the intercessor that is important in prayers for healing, as well as, laying-on-hands.

Jesus said, "Everything you ask for in prayer, if you have faith, you will receive (Matthew 21:22 Phillips). This is a rather explicit promise and I know personally through many experiences, that when we apply faith and work within God's natural laws, the truth of this promise is known.

When all the conditions are met and physical healing does not occur, then the question of why some are healed and some are not raises many doubts concerning the validity of spiritual healing.

It is true that when all conditions are right, healing may or may not occur physically, but we can always be assured that healing of the spirit has occurred. This is the beauty and wonder of the art of spiritual healing.

Following a healing of the spirit, when death comes, it is always a peaceful passing. To be spiritually healed is of vital importance to eternal life with the Father.

Recently this every experience happened to a very nice gentleman who was suffering rapid paralysis from Lou Gehrig's disease. After three visits for healing he had a mystical experience with Christ and knew the real meaning of being filled with a peace that passes all understanding. The peace remained with him through his passing. This was the healing of his spirit even though the physical body was not healed.

It is of far greater importance to be spiritually healed than to be physically healed, as we all must eventually die a physical death, but the soul is eternal and lives on seeking ultimate oneness with God.

Healing was the major part of Jesus Christ's ministry and is therefore a part of the foundation of the Christian faith. It is the greatest example of God's gift of eternal love and will ever remain

His mystical secret.

7 EPILOGUE

As I reflect on these years of change, and this endeavor to share my experiences, I realize that there is as much left unsaid as has been said. I was not aware, when I began this book, that it would be very difficult for me to share these very personal experiences. The Holy Spirit has led me ever so gently into this writing, in the same way I was led gently and subtly into a healing ministry. This is an example of what can happen when self will is surrendered to live within His Divine Will.

Living life on a spiritual path brings more blessings than could ever be thought possible.

It is thought by many that to surrender self to live within Gods will would be to give up the pleasures of life; however, just the opposite is true. As a commitment is made to live within His will, even just one day at a time, and to whatever degree this may be, the desires that once were thought to bring pleasure gradually fade away if they were not to the highest good possible.

It is never necessary to sacrifice anything; for example, trying to stop smoking or whatever undesirable habit that needs to be broken. The only requirement is to seek attunement with God within, and with the sincere desire to try to live within His will; all else eventually falls into place.

When the spiritual life is entered all other things are added. God is the source of all peace, joy, health, supply and love. When we allow Him to manifest through us, we then experience inner change and our outward conditions become smoother and harmonious as if by magic.

To know Inner peace after years of fear and anxiety is so marvelous that it defies description. "I leave behind with you - peace; I give you my own peace and my gift is nothing like the peace of this world" (John 14:21 Phillips).

As we practice His Presence through the Silence of meditation, peace replaces fear and all of the other negative emotions that act as barriers to His Grace and the Kingdom.

At some point in time all must be lifted from the human level of consciousness into spiritual awareness, and this can be achieved now by those who have the desire and patience to learn and practice meditation. We may have knowledge of God, but not know God as the Spirit that dwells within us all. This requires a personal experience that is found in the Silence of meditation.

God within is the "I am that I am." It is the God within who "stands at the door and knocks" at the door of our consciousness. We have but to seek sincerely and we shall find Him within. Then we enter the Kingdom and live the spiritual life where there is no fear and anxiety and all our needs are met abundantly.

Reading of other's spiritual lives is helpful but until there is a burning desire within the individual to seek spiritual experience it remains only knowledge. Wisdom comes from applying knowledge, and it is through this application that the spiritual path is begun.

The Spiritual path that all must take at some point in eternity is the soul's ultimate journey to union with God. The purpose and necessity of the path is for purging and purification of the soul, preparing it for union in Perfect Love with God.

Living the spiritual life does not mean that all problems will suddenly disappear, they may even become worse, depending on what needs to be purged. The difference is that attitudes concerning problems are changed as problems are viewed as opportunities for inner growth.

It has been through the understanding of the law of cause and effect, as this law relates to problems, that has been my greatest victory. My mind is in a constant state of thanksgiving for each problem and crisis that ultimately led me to this spiritual quest. Without these very problems that I once moaned and groaned over, I would still be spiritually dead. Joseph Smith said, "If there is no conflict, I cannot gain a victory; if there is no victory, I cannot gain a crown of reward."

It was through a recent crisis that I discovered my crown of reward. It is just not possible to really know the depth of our faith until our inner strength is tested through conflict. A soldier never knows his strength until he meets his foe. During the past twelve years of my quest, my family's life has been relatively free of any major upheavals, and though I knew that I had the inner strength to handle any situation, it had not been put to the test.

Last summer I was given the opportunity to have my inner strength and faith tested, and to apply the teachings that I had learned on the spiritual path. It was a very real time of testing for me, as I faced the first real crisis since my quest had begun.

My husband lost his business and we suffered a great financial loss. This was quite a blow to us as the future had looked so financially bright and promising.

This was a dark night of the soul for me as I struggled to apply all that I had learned concerning God and His spiritual laws and thereby rise above the problems.

It is in these times of testing that we can feel forsaken and quite alone. But through this feeling of being forsaken, it is possible to learn to draw upon the inner Source and know that His Grace is sufficient. On the cross Jesus said, "My God my God, why did you forsake me?" (Matthew 27:46 Phillips).

Even our Master felt this emotion in his own dark night of the soul, His crucifixion.

As I have come to realize through past problems and crises, these are blessings for the purpose of growth, and this one was no exception. This financial problem resulted in a deeper understanding, insight, and growth for me and my husband. Through this I found that I had not completely released my need for financial security in absolute trust that God would provide for every need. Our needs may not be what they seem to be in our finite minds, but He does provide for every need when we allow His Spirit to manifest as our supply. This requires faith, and the ability to let the problem go as it is released to God in prayer. He said to take no anxious thought and I have found that as I was able to surrender this financial problem to Him, my faith has been strengthened.

Things have worked out beautifully for us and there have been many side blessings. Our family was brought even closer together through this financial setback as we all pitched in together and learned how to be more frugal. It was so wonderful to see our son and daughter come up with realistic suggestions for economizing. Through this Bob has found a deeper relationship with God, and our marriage has been strengthened so that after twenty-five years of marriage we are closer now than ever before.

We credit the closeness, possibly even the survival of our marriage to the spiritual path and the transformation of my life. Bob told me, "Since you have been on the spiritual path, you have become easier to get along with." As I have tried to impart, this is spiritual law in operation. As an inner change is experienced, then the environment changes to the same degree.

Today my security is founded in a deep and abiding faith that is the result of many experiences along a spiritual path, and of trial and error in human judgment as I struggled to discern Divine guidance from my own personal self will.

When a spiritual quest is undertaken, the first question usually asked is, "How do I know the difference between the conscious mind and inner guidance?" This is extremely difficult at first, as most of us have always depended strictly on human logic to solve problems and make decisions. It is a fact that the human consciousness will usually argue with the inner direction. I recall once, shortly after we moved into our new home five years ago, that as I went out of the door, leaving it unlocked, something urged me to lock the door. In our previous home we were accustomed to always leaving the doors unlocked while away for quick errands, but here in our new home we had decided to make it a policy to always lock the doors when we left. Well, I argued with myself that I would only be gone fifteen minutes, and it was ridiculous to go back and lock the door for such a short time. Upon returning, fifteen minutes later, I found two teenage boys running away, their arms loaded. An extremely valuable coin collection was taken, along with a few other things.

At this time I knew how to discern the difference between inner direction and human consciousness, but there is something about human will that makes "letting go and letting God" so very difficult. From the cradle we are taught to be independent, and as independent adults it seems normal to feel that there is not anything that cannot be accomplished when we set our minds to the task.

The ego gets in the way as we try to change this life pattern and give up our own little self wills. Being a strong willed person myself, this has been very difficult. I have thought at times that I was certainly doing His will only to find that I really was still trudging right along my own way.

It takes deep desire, commitment, and practice to live everyday in His will. There is a new hymn out that says, "Just one day at a time, sweet Jesus." It is much easier to start trying to discern His will one day at a time, and it can become a fun thing as the schedule becomes completely altered from what was originally planned. And this is not a frustration, as it might appear to be but a very satisfying experience when it is recognized that the changed schedule is more rewarding than the original schedule.

In reflecting on the many changes that have occurred in my life during the past twelve years, and I consider these years a miracle in themselves, the greatest miracle has been the gift of healing.

It still astounds me that God could use even me. This was an area that I knew nothing about and had never even remotely considered the subject one way or the other. Even after several healing experiences, just what it all meant was still not clear to me. It is amazing how far afield we can get from His Divine purpose, and how equally amazing to find how simple it all seems after starting upon a spiritual quest.

My healing ministry is the source of the greatest joy that I have ever known, and also the producer of much heartache. To witness someone healed is witnessing the Holy Spirit in action, and it is breathtaking. There are really no words that are adequate to describe such a mystical experience. The other side is the sharing of the disappointment of the one who is not healed, and feeling so helpless through it all.

An experience of healing brings a knowledge of God and a deeper relationship with Him. The knowledge that God is the Source of life And offers to everyone inner peace and wholeness is vital to the life of the Church and to human life.

Being a channel for healing is an enormous responsibility, and one that I take very seriously. In recent weeks several people have called who want to be healers and ask how I happened to get started, and what might be suggested for them. Since this was not my idea, and I have done nothing to promote it, I could be of little help, except to say that it is extremely important to discern inner guidance and be very sure that the course taken is the right direction. It is then that doors will open, and the way will be made clear without any personal effort. So it is when we allow His purpose and will to manifest itself in our lives.

The Church is the natural place for a healing ministry and there is a desperate need for this as more and more people are becoming aware that there is something lacking in their lives today.

It has been my experience as I talk to church groups that there is little or no awareness that Christ does heal today and that everyone can have a personal relationship with God without being a fanatic.

What is lacking in the Church today is the individual's personal relationship with God. This problem could be easily solved with an effective healing ministry in the Church. The Church is often uncomfortable with the mystical side of religion and I am acutely aware of this in my present position. However, with the growing interest of many persons both inside and outside the Church, the tide is turning and I believe that in this lifetime we will see a spiritual revolution that will turn the hearts of mankind back to God.

For many, life is all too often a constant struggle to gain material possessions while at the same time trying to attain spiritual values. While there is much concern in protecting personal property with warranties, the only real and lasting protection needed is the warranty to live as we covenant our lives with God.

Editor's Note: *About the time my mother was completing this book, the country went into an economic recession that ruined my father's construction business. Many will recall the recession of 1974, and the OPEC oil embargo which created skyrocketing prices, fuel shortages, and long gas station lines. My father took a job with a construction company in Houston, Texas which had him traveling frequently to a building site in Las Vegas, Nevada. My parents put their house on the market with plans to move to*

Houston, but with the recession going on there were no buyers. Dad was only able to return to Atlanta, and spend time with the family once a month. He was very lonely, and after a year of being on the road, he had a stroke. When that happened, my mother's healing ministry came to a halt. She needed to take care of my father, as well as, go back to work as an X-ray technician in order to pay bills. With all of that going on, this book - although finished - was put aside and forgotten.

Life's Lessons

by John Henry Newman

I learn as the years roll onward

And leave the past behind.

That much I have counted sorrow

But proves our God is kind.

That many a flower I longed for

Had a hidden thorn of pain,

And many a rugged bypath

Led to fields of ripened grain.

The clouds that cover the sunshine

They cannot banish the Sun,

And the earth shines out the brighter

When the weary rain is done.

We must stand in the deepest shadow

To see the clearest light;

And often from wrong's own darkness

Comes the weary strength of right.

We must live through the weary winter

If we would value the spring.

And the woods must be cold and silent,

Before the robins sing.

The flowers must be buried in darkness

Before they can bud and bloom,

And the sweetest and warmest sunshine

Comes after the storm and gloom.

So the heart from the hardest trial gains

The purest joy of all,

And from the Lips that have tasted sadness

The sweetest songs will fall,

For as peace comes after suffering,

And love is reward of pain.

So after earth comes heaven,

And out of our loss the gain.

8 SUGGESTED READING

I. Allen, James. As A Man Thinketh. Kansas City, Missouri: Hallmark Cards, Inc, 1968.

Kampis, Thomas a. The Imitation of Christ. Cleveland, Ohio: The World Publishing Company, 1969.

Bach, Marcus. The Inner Ecstasy. Nashville, Tennessee: Abingdon Press, 1969.

Eggleston, Louise. Prayer Series and Subconscious Series. Norfolk, Virginia: World Literacy Prayer Group, 1961.

Fox, Emmet. The Sermon on the Mount. New York: Harper and Row, 1934.

Fromm, Erich. The Art of Loving. New York: Harper and Row, 1956.

Goldsmith, Joel. The Art of Meditation. New York: Harper and Row, 1956.

Goldsmith, Joel. The Art of Spiritual Healing. New York: Harper and Row, 1959.

Hutschnecker, Arnold. The Will to Live. Englewood Cliffs, New Jersey: Prentice-Hall, 1951.

Kelsey, Morton. Healing and Christianity. New York: Harper and Row, 1973.

Kimmel, Jo, Steps to Prayer Power. Nashville, Tennessee: Abingdon Press, 1972.

Laubach, Frank, Prayer, The Mightiest Force in the World. Old Tappan, New Jersey: Fleming H. Revell, 1946.

Maclachlan, Lewis. Common Sense About Prayer. London, England: James Clarke and Co., Ltd., 1965.

Maclachlan, Lewis. How to Pray for Healing. London, England: James Clarke and Co., 1955.

Parker, William. Prayer Can Change Your Life. Englewood Cliffs, New Jersey: Prentice-Hall, 1957.

Sanford, Agnes. The Healing Light. St. Paul, Minnesota: Macalester Park, 1947.

Sanford, Agnes. Behold Your God. St. Paul, Minnesota: Macalester Park, 1958.

Sanford, John. The Kingdom Within. Philadelphia, Pennsylvania: Lippincott, 1970.

Sherman, Harold. How to Use the Power of Prayer, New York: C and R Anthony, Inc., 1958.

Sherman, Harold. How to Make ESP Work for You. New York: Fawcett Crest, 1967.

Steadman, Alice. Who's the Matter with Me. Lakemont, Georgia: CSA Press, 1971.

Tournier, Paul. The Healing of Persons. New York: Harper and Row, 1965.

Tournier, Paul. The Meaning of Persons. New York: Harper and Row, 1973.

Tournier, Paul. The Strong and the Weak. Philadelphia, Pennsylvania: Westminster Press, 1963.

Turner, Gordon, An Outline of Spiritual Healing. London, England: Psychic Press, 1970.

Weatherhead, Leslie. Life Begins at Death. Nashville, Tennessee: Abingdon Press, 1969.

Weatherhead, Leslie. The Will of God. Nashville, Tennessee; Abingdon Press, 1944.

White, Anne. Healing Adventure. Plainfield, New Jersey; Logos International, 1972.

ABOUT THE AUTHOR

Barbara Wilson was born in Savannah, Georgia. She grew up during the Great Depression and World War II. After graduating high school, she studied x-ray technology at Georgia Baptist Hospital. When she was 19 years old, she married Robert Wilson. Shortly thereafter, they moved to Atlanta, Georgia where she would live for the rest of her life. They had two children: Robert Jr. and Cynthia.

www.ingramcontent.com/pod-product-compliance
Lightning Source LLC
Chambersburg PA
CBHW071417040426
42445CB00012BA/1195